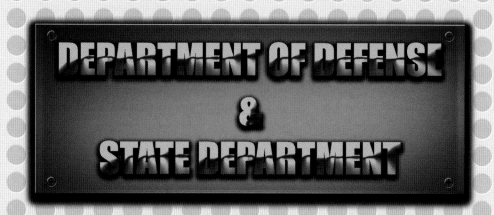

DEPARTMENT OF DEFENSE & STATE DEPARTMENT

FIGHTING TERRORISM

David Baker

Rourke

Publishing LLC
Vero Beach, Florida 32964

www.rourkepublishing.com

PHOTO CREDITS: p. 34: AFP/Getty Images; p. 38: CNN/Getty Images; p. 30: Corbis; pp. 5, 19 (Jim Garramone), 35 (Jim Wagner), 37: Department of Defense; pp. 8, 12: Chris Fairclough/Chris Fairclough Worldwide Ltd; p. 20: Khaled Fkirien/Panapress/Getty Images; p. 21: Ramzi Haidar/AFP/Getty Images; p. 18: Sam Kittner/National Geographic/ Getty Images; pp. 14, 15, 29, 33: Library of Congress; p. 40: Shah Marai/AFP/ Getty Images; pp. 16, 26: MPI/Getty Images; p. 9: Mike Nelson/AFP/Getty Images; p. 32: Peter Newark's Military Pictures; p. 42: Mandel Ngan/AFP/Getty Images; p. 10: SANA/Getty Images; p. 6: Pascal Le Segretain/Getty Images; p. 17: Three Lions/Getty Images; pp. 4 (Tech. Sgt. Andy Dunaway), 22 (Staff Sgt. Jeromy K. Cross), 43 (Tech. Sgt. Jerry Morrison Jr.): U.S. Air Force; p. 39 (Staff Sgt. Joseph P. Collins Jr.): U.S. Army; p. 23 (James Tourtellotte): U.S. Customs & Border Protection; pp. 27, 28: U.S. Military Academy; p. 25 (Photographer's Mate 2nd Class Damon J. Moritz): U.S. Navy

Title page picture shows recruits in training at the U.S. Naval Academy in Annapolis.

Produced for Rourke Publishing by Discovery Books
Editor: Paul Humphrey
Designer: Ian Winton
Photo researcher: Rachel Tisdale

Library of Congress Cataloging-in-Publication Data

Baker, David, 1944-
   Department of Defense and State Department / by David Baker.
      p. cm. -- (Fighting terrorism)
   Includes index.
   ISBN 1-59515-483-3
   1. United States--Defenses--Juvenile literature. 2. Civil defense--United States--Juvenile literature. 3. United States. Dept. of Defense--Juvenile literature. 4. United States. Dept. of State--Juvenile literature. 5. United States--Foreign relations--2001---Juvenile literature. 6. War on Terrorism, 2001---Juvenile literature. I. Title.
   UA23.B243 2006
   363.320973--dc22
                                    2005028174
Printed in the USA

TABLE OF CONTENTS

Chapter One

Representing the Nation

The headquarters of the Department of Defense is the Pentagon building, in Arlington, Virginia.

The U. S. government has many important roles to play on behalf of its citizens. Some of these are that it should preserve and protect the interests and liberties of the people, defend the nation against attack, and conduct itself in a civilized manner before all other nations on earth. Preservation and the protection of interests is conducted through a wide range of government departments that look after the education, welfare, and the work and health rights of its citizens.

Condoleezza Rice became secretary of state in January 2005.

Defense of the nation and its people is the responsibility of organizations like the Federal Bureau of Investigation (FBI), the Central Intelligence Agency (CIA), and the Department of Defense.

Representation of the United States to other countries is the work of the Department of State, and it is one of the most important functions of the government. It is the one agency through which other countries communicate their interests and intentions to the U.S. government and get responses back in return. The Department of State has a long history, one that has changed considerably over the more than 200 years since independence.

Chapter Two

The Department of State

The State Department has several unique roles and many duties to perform. Today it is responsible for looking after U.S. citizens abroad and providing them with the full protection of

the government as if they were in their own country. It is also the section of government responsible for discussing agreements between the United States and other countries and forging special relations and friendly links for the benefit of all. Negotiations and agreements are carried out by **diplomats** who receive their instructions from senior officers in government—right up to the Office of the President.

Policy is made by a cabinet of senior politicians and by the **administration**, whose policy is carried out by the State Department. It is also the department responsible for receiving foreigners into the United States, checking their identities as a means of detecting those wishing to enter the country who could do harm through either criminal or terrorist activity.

The history of the State Department mirrors the history of our nation. Over the last 200 years the nation has been challenged to rise against great threats and serve the cause of fundamental beliefs in the rights of all people wherever they may live. Toward that end American diplomacy against countries practicing **oppression** has been focused around persuasion and pressure: persuasion through diplomacy and pressure through the use of trade restrictions and **embargoes**.

(Opposite) The U.S. Embassy in Rabat, Morocco. The State Department is responsible for negotiating with all foreign governments.

7

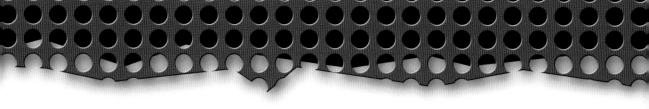

Chapter Three

Understanding the World

The world today is a complex place. More than 200 countries have their own people, government, and policies. The United States is the richest and the most powerful country in the world. Because of that many countries want to do business with

Sometimes diplomacy is successful in removing ruthless dictators, but for others, like Iraq's Saddam Hussein, more forceful methods sometimes have to be used.

America, and people from other countries frequently visit its great sights and tourist attractions. It is the job of the State Department to adapt policies to a changing world in which **globalization** brings wealth and prosperity to many.

The expanding exchange of ideas and trade is believed to stimulate political changes that take place in countries run by **dictators** or **autocrats**. Such countries frequently imprison their own people, carry out terrible **atrocities** against individuals

(Opposite) Tourists in New York City. The State Department is responsible for checking that people entering the country from abroad are not criminals or terrorists.

Sometimes it is necessary, in the interests of world peace, for the secretary of state to meet with heads of government our government disapproves of. Here Secretary Colin Powell meets with Syrian President Bashar al-Assad (left), May 2003.

who want a free society, and put in prison those who advocate democracy. Most people in countries with developed societies believe there is a moral right in working to help others in the world to become free from oppression and to support freedom wherever it is in peril.

Some nations realize that the advantages of joining the majority of countries that support freedom and the rights of individuals are great. Conforming to moral and **ethical** standards and working peacefully with other countries bring great benefits of partnerships, cooperation, and trade. This does not always occur, but the United States has for the last several decades adopted a policy of education and assistance to help newly developing countries seek a peaceful route through their difficulties.

This is an important step toward preventing the rise of terrorism. The diplomatic discussions that take place between countries help reduce levels of tension. There is no substitute for sitting down with a potentially hostile leader and discussing possible options for greater understanding and reconciliation. Nobody likes being told what to do by somebody you did not ask for help. That is not the purpose of the State Department.

If the Department of Defense is the "police" agency, with the purpose of stopping terrorists from threatening U.S. interests, the State Department is the negotiator that seeks to keep the "bad" guy from firing first. The reaction is sometimes hostile. Occasionally it is welcomed. In fact, the State Department works as a sort of shield, seeking to **stabilize** tension and protecting people from aggression and the worst effects of international violence. This is done through a global system of **embassies** in which **ambassadors** convey the wishes and policies of the U.S. government and receive instructions on policy and position in return. In this way a **dialogue** exists through which **negotiation** can reduce tension, create a closer relationship between countries, and serve as a **conduit** for discussion.

The Department of State through its network of embassies provides aid and other assistance to the world's poorest people, like these schoolchildren in Kenya.

Chapter Four

Developing a Dialogue

The State Department is one of the oldest branches of the U.S. government and was patterned on Britain's secretary of state for foreign affairs. It was with great reluctance that the Congressional Congress approved a department that would handle discussions with foreign countries. Benjamin Franklin, one of the most distinguished Americans of his day, was the first American diplomat. From 1776 to 1778 he served on a three-man **commission** to France and gained French support for the War of Independence. In 1779 he became the first American Minister (the equivalent of an ambassador).

John Adams represented America in France from 1778 to 1779, but returned to Paris in 1780 as a peace commissioner with responsibility to the Congress for settling conflict between the United States and Great Britain. He had no luck trying to achieve that and moved to Holland as Minister to the Netherlands. Believing the Dutch to be conspiring with the Americans, Britain declared war on Holland in December 1780. Fearing attack from the British Navy on their trade with America, the Dutch were reluctant to side with the newly

Benjamin Franklin was America's first diplomat. Here he is shown with King Louis XVI of France in March 1778.

independent country. Nevertheless, Adams successfully negotiated a loan from the Dutch, which saved the United States from **bankruptcy**, and in 1782 the Dutch finally granted it full recognition.

For the newly liberated **colonies** the value of negotiation and foreign diplomacy was a great advantage, even if few of the Congressmen fully understood that fact. It was help in a very practical way that helped save the American Revolution. In 1781 the 8,000-strong French army joined American units totaling the same number and defeated the British forces at the battle of Yorktown.

For three years the French troops and naval forces had supported the hard-pressed Continental Army since the signing of treaties of alliance between America and France on February 6, 1778.

In 1782 Benjamin Franklin declined a British offer for peace on the grounds of some measure of independence for the 13 colonies. Instead he held out for full independence and full recognition by the British. After two months of negotiations, the British finally accepted terms, and peace with America was signed on November 30, 1782 and with France on September 3, 1783. It was the end of a long road during which negotiation had brought several countries

Thomas Jefferson succeeded Benjamin Franklin in 1785. He became America's third president in 1801.

THOMAS JEFFERSON.
Third President of the United States

An artist's drawing of the surrender of British forces at Yorktown, Virginia, October 17, 1781.

to the aid of the new Congress and was an important part of making the United States an independent nation.

With peace came opportunity for organizing a government fit to administer the new nation. Motivated by independence from the motherland, people wanted assurance that they would not be plunged into foreign wars.

A new Department of State was needed to look after their concerns, to properly represent the nation overseas, and to control the **immigration** of people from other countries. At first it was called the Department of Foreign Affairs when Congress voted it into being on July 27, 1789. Less than two months later it got the name it carries to this day, and the Department of State became an integral part of the administration of the American nation.

When founded, the State Department was also approved as **custodian** of all the enacted laws of the country, records of Congress, and the Constitution as well as the Declaration of Independence. Since then it has had to support the expansion and development of the United States both as a strong and progressive nation and as a major global power. Through two world wars it sought to help bring peace and, once acquired, to maintain it. Now there are other matters that are expanding the role of the State Department.

The signing of the Treaty of Paris, a peace treaty between the United States and Great Britain that concluded the American War of Independence.

Chapter Five

New Challenges

In addition to representing the interests of the United States, the government is also active in helping stimulate global cooperation to tackle universal problems affecting most people wherever they live. Two of the most pressing problems are **environmental pollution** and the threat from terrorism.

The aftermath of the September 11, 2001 terrorist attack on the Pentagon. Tackling world terrorism is now the number one task for the U.S. State Department.

The State Department has special offices that seek to encourage global cooperation in the fight against pollution by negotiating science-based treaties with other countries. By combining globalization with environmental concerns, the United States hopes to unite domestic interests with those of other countries. This movement of such issues into mainstream foreign policy is known as Environmental Diplomacy.

Removing the threat from terrorism is harder to achieve. Most people want clean air and water and less pollution, but not all countries are agreed on the way to tackle terrorism. Unpleasant as it is, some countries fund terrorist groups and provide shelter and protection for groups of individuals that

(Opposite) Smoke billows from an oil refinery in Baton Rouge, Louisiana. Global pollution is a world threat requiring skillful diplomacy by the Department of State.

Colonel Muammar al Qaddafi, the Libyan leader, has frequently supported international terrorist groups in the past.

threaten free democratic processes in other places. They literally "export" terrorism and rarely admit responsibility. Combating this is one important part of the work carried out by the State Department through its embassies abroad.

It has a Counterterrorism Office that uses all available means to bring terrorists to justice. The Office also isolates and applies pressure to states that provide **safe haven** for terrorists and works with other countries that need help to stop the spread of terrorism or to seek out terrorists within their own borders.

Through the State Department many countries work cooperatively with the United States to assist their own security services to combine resources in this new war on international violence and terror. People, technology, and laws help the fight against terror, and the State Department is at the center of it all.

Unlike conventional conflict where countries declare themselves to be friend or foe,

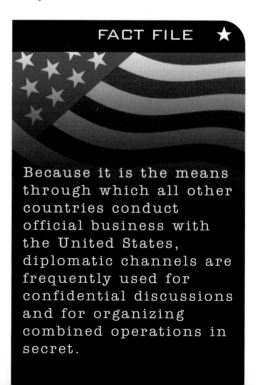

FACT FILE ★

Because it is the means through which all other countries conduct official business with the United States, diplomatic channels are frequently used for confidential discussions and for organizing combined operations in secret.

terrorist groups sometimes work secretly inside their own or other countries because they can hide and escape detection. When such groups are discovered to be on their territory, these countries often ask for help from outside, adding to the level of cooperation and improving the chances of detecting the terrorist groups. This level of assistance provided by the United States can sometimes involve the CIA, and sometimes it involves the Department of Defense. Either way, the State Department can channel the appropriate response to the relevant department or agency.

The Hezbollah terrorist group has long been supported by the Iranian government. The group is dedicated to the overthrow of the Jewish state of Israel.

The need for U.S. government departments to work closely with each other means a central authority can make balanced decisions about what to do and how to do it. Accordingly, in November 2004 President George W. Bush appointed an Acting Coordinator for Counterterrorism to work with all U.S. government departments and with foreign governments as well in this unifying effort. Such cooperation would be impossible without the services of the State Department.

Secretary of State Condoleezza Rice greets U.S. embassy and other military personnel at the American Embassy in Baghdad, Iraq, on May 15, 2005.

Because it is able to work with governments and official agencies in other countries, the State Department can operate directly with the permission of the authorities to provide assistance and aid. With terrorism come casualties, and although there have been many attacks on U.S. embassies and other buildings, including those of American companies, the dead and wounded that result from acts of violence can often include people from countries other than the United States.

One example is the terrible sequence of events of September 11, 2001, when more than 3,000 people, citizens of 36 countries, were killed when four airplanes were **hijacked** and brought down, two on the World Trade Center Twin Towers in New York City, one on the Pentagon near Washington, D.C., and a fourth by passengers before reaching its target. Each of these 36 countries suffered at the hands of terrorists willing to lose their own lives in the act of killing others in large number.

Each of the 36 countries and many more helped provide the State Department with information leading to the identity and possible arrest of suspects planning further atrocities. More than that, however, the State Department plays a direct role in casualty assistance and in helping people, young and old, come to terms with grief and the loss of a loved one. U.S. government workers, and those from other democratic countries, themselves run the risk of attack. The State Department has a special office for casualty assistance and for guiding the recovery of survivors who can be severely affected by their harrowing experience, both physically and mentally.

The ruins of the World Trade Center Twin Towers following the terrorist attacks on September 11, 2001. People from many countries were killed by this outrage.

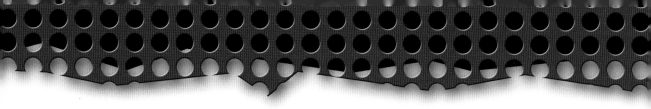

Chapter Six

The Department of Defense

When diplomatic means to achieve peaceful solutions fail, it is sometimes necessary to use force. Many times in the past, the United States has had to use its military strength to defeat enemies and dictators determined to destroy America or its allies. At other times a strong military force is useful to deter aggression before the fighting starts. Some people believe this is a way to keep the peace. By maintaining strong and highly professional defense forces potential enemies could be deterred, they say, and a war prevented by showing strength and a determination to fight if necessary.

Defense forces can also be used to hunt down terrorist organizations and to go to war against countries determined to wage war through terrorist activity. Today, we rely on our armed forces to defend the nation, protect its citizens, and deter aggression wherever possible. It has not always been like that, and the history of our defense forces explains why they have a special and vital role to play in the modern world. To appreciate that, it is necessary to understand the role they played in the past.

The Department of Defense has overall responsibility for all the nation's military forces. Here, at the U.S. Naval Academy in Annapolis, a squad of recruits works with a log as part of teamwork training during sea trials.

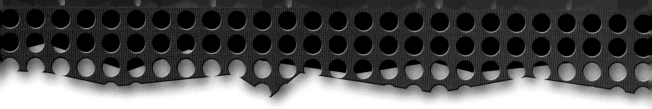

Chapter Seven

Defending Freedom

For a long time after the War of Independence, the United States maintained only a small professional army and navy. During the colonial period before independence, citizens had relied on the British army and the navy to protect them from the French and the Spanish. After independence, a small Continental

The U.S. Military Academy as it appeared in 1828, just 26 years after it was founded.

Army of paid professional soldiers was supplemented by a volunteer force drawn from a wide range of farmers and laborers. In addition, in 1798 the Marine Corps was set up under the command of the secretary of the navy to conduct land operations essential to seaborne warfare.

Efforts were made to build a professional officer class when the U.S. Military Academy at West Point was established in 1802. A Naval School was opened at Annapolis in 1845 and renamed the U.S. Naval Academy in 1850—the name it holds to this day. For several decades these forces were used very little, and successive governments only employed the professional soldiers to put down Indian uprisings in the west.

(Opposite) At the end of the War of Independence only a small army was maintained to defend the nation. This picture shows the disbanding of the Continental Army at war's end, November 1783.

Cadets training at the West Point Military Academy, at West Point, New York, today.

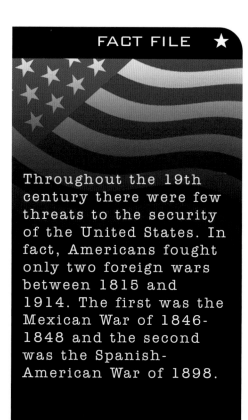

Then came the war in Europe, usually known as World War I. Between 1914 and 1918 European countries fought each other for the preservation of boundaries and their own national identity. In 1917, under President Woodrow Wilson, the United States went to the aid of the French, the British, and the Italians against the combined forces of Germany and Austria-Hungary.

By November 1918 an **armistice** had been signed, in

President Woodrow Wilson took the United States into World War I in 1917. The war ended the following year.

which the combatant countries agreed to meet at Versailles, France, to agree to a permanent settlement. That agreement was reached in 1919. Following the war America almost completely disarmed, believing that World War I had been a "war to end all wars." This was not the case, however, and America began to rebuild her armed forces when dictators seized power in Italy and Germany.

The Nazi dictator Adolf Hitler invaded neighboring Poland in September of 1939. Just three weeks later the Soviet leader Josef Stalin attacked Poland, and between them the two dictators carved up this ancient European country for themselves. In May 1940 Hitler attacked western Europe, including France, and Italy joined in as German bombers **blitzed** Great Britain.

Holding out against the Axis powers—Germany and Italy—Great Britain gained help from America until the United States

American troops raise the flag after liberating the island of Iwo Jima from the Japanese in February 1945, the year World War II ended.

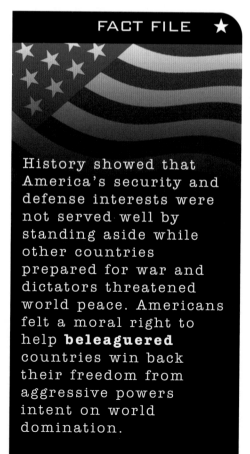

FACT FILE ★

History showed that America's security and defense interests were not served well by standing aside while other countries prepared for war and dictators threatened world peace. Americans felt a moral right to help **beleaguered** countries win back their freedom from aggressive powers intent on world domination.

was forced to enter the war. On December 7, 1941, less than six months after Hitler invaded Russia, Japan brutally attacked the U.S. naval base at Pearl Harbor, Hawaii, propelling America into what was to become World War II. For more than three years, American armed forces fought back, first helping defeat Hitler in Europe and then against the Japanese occupation of Pacific islands, finally bringing about the surrender of all Japanese forces in September 1945.

Chapter Eight

A New Defense

After the war America maintained strong armed forces and reorganized for new threats that appeared to come from the Soviet Union (also called the USSR, or sometimes just Russia). Although America and the USSR had been allies during World War II, Russia was a **communist** state and tried to influence free elections in European countries liberated from Nazi occupation. The USSR wanted to encourage as many countries as possible to choose communism over democracy and used violence in an attempt to achieve this, threatening the very existence of the United States.

Under the leadership of President Harry S. Truman, a new Department of Defense was formed in 1947. In addition to a Department of the Army and a Department of the Navy, there was now a Department of the Air Force—an independent Air Force separated from control by the army. The Marine Corps was retained as the fourth U.S. military service. The new Department of Defense was based in the Pentagon, a building just outside Washington, DC.

As tensions between America and the USSR increased into

what became the Cold War, some countries sought to bring about the collapse of democracy by attacking U.S. interests around the world. With America seemingly preoccupied—helping small nations resist pressure from the Soviet Union to adopt communism—other countries were intent on undermining free speech and democracy. Many groups opposed to western-style democracy picked up weapons as the only means they saw by which they could make their point.

Increasingly, terrorism began to emerge as a means of using violence in an attempt to frighten countries keen to work with the United States. American citizens working abroad were attacked and American buildings—such as embassies, U.S. companies with factories overseas, and military establishments—were attacked as a means of protest but also in attempts to bring pressure for Americans to leave.

The Russian flag is hoisted over the German parliament building in Berlin, May 1945. Soon Germany, and much of Europe, was to be divided between the democratic west and communist east.

President Harry S. Truman was charged with containing the worldwide threat of communism after World War II.

The governments of several countries secretly funded terrorists, gave them protection and safety, or hid them from security organizations. From these host countries, terrorists would learn techniques for making bombs, carrying out assassinations, disrupting communications and transportation, or simply distributing anti-American propaganda. Some would raise money for the terrorist groups while others would learn how to **infiltrate** democratic countries and recruit new members for terrorist purposes. By the 1970s terrorism was becoming a major problem for Americans and their allies in the world.

The U.S. State Department and the Department of Defense worked closely together to identify terrorist organizations, groups that supported terrorists, and others that were sympathizers. It was sometimes possible to identify the terrorists, and over time several leaders stood out and were named. These men and women used countries sympathetic to their causes to hide away until they could attack. It was as though the world's most powerful intelligence and security organization was chasing shadows in dark places, unable to hunt them down or root them out.

Plane hijacking as a means of terrorism emerged in the 1970s. This picture shows the remains of three planes that were hijacked and then blown up in Jordan in September 1970.

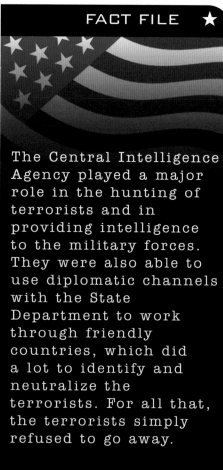

FACT FILE ★

The Central Intelligence Agency played a major role in the hunting of terrorists and in providing intelligence to the military forces. They were also able to use diplomatic channels with the State Department to work through friendly countries, which did a lot to identify and neutralize the terrorists. For all that, the terrorists simply refused to go away.

Because the State Department and the Defense Department represented the greatest single number of Americans living and working overseas, they were frequently involved as targets. They were also best placed to identify and hunt down the terrorists themselves. Close **liaison** between these U.S. government organizations was essential in helping suppress outrageous aggression and murder.

Chapter Nine

Defense against Terror

Defending Americans against terrorism is not only about good intelligence and knowing when and where terrorists are going to attack. Sometimes it is necessary to go out and fight them directly. Some terrorist groups have grown into groups of several hundred people, with a further following of several thousand who sympathize with them. In these proportions terrorist groups can operate like armies, and it is necessary to use battlefield tactics to suppress them.

Over the decades U.S. military forces have developed equipment to find and attack terrorist groups wherever they may be. In some cases this has led to major air, land, or sea

Before the U.S and coalition forces invaded Afghanistan in 2001, it was ruled by the Taliban, a ruthless group who supported Islamic terrorism. Here, a U.S. infantryman captures a member of the Taliban in March 2003.

strikes against terrorist camps and hideaways known as **enclaves**.

Weapons are selected according to the target, and attacks are organized to reduce civilian casualties to a minimum. Sometimes this is not possible, and an attack upon an entire country is needed to defeat the terrorists. When actions like these are conducted, it sometimes leads to neighboring states siding with American forces and cooperating across borders. One example of that was the assault on Afghanistan to seek out the terrorist group Al Qaeda led by Osama bin Laden.

After the events of September 11, 2001, when airliners were turned into bombs against New York and Washington, it was clear that Osama bin Laden had conducted plans for the attacks from his mountain bases in Afghanistan. The CIA and the Defense Department had been watching this group for several years. Top secret satellites were used to listen to communications between known terrorists, and pictures were taken of locations where they were training suicide bombers.

These satellites had been developed by government agencies responsible for gathering highly **classified** information about potential enemies of the United States. One of these agencies—the National Reconnaissance Office—had led the way toward highly advanced systems launched by rockets from Cape Canaveral, Florida. The technical development of satellites had taken place during

FACT FILE ★

Satellites using conventional but powerful cameras could only take images during daylight and through clear skies. **Radar** satellites took pictures using radar beams and were able to produce images almost as good as conventional pictures—at night and through clouds or fog.

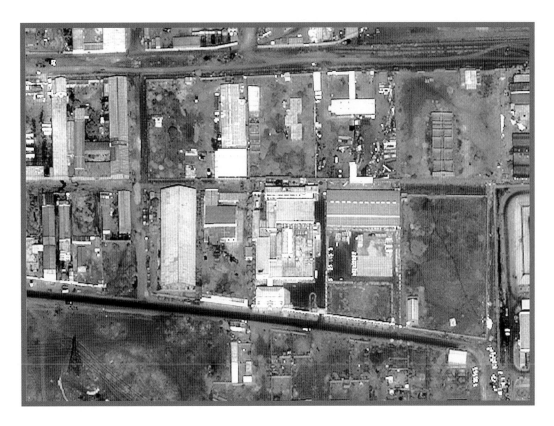

Aerial photographs like this one, of a suspected chemical weapons plant in the Sudan, are useful in finding information about the activities of countries hostile to the United States.

the Cold War. This resulted in the use of sophisticated space-based systems, known as "assets," which could be used to gather large amounts of information about countries, states, and even individuals.

After the Cold War ended, the rise in terrorism encouraged further development of these sophisticated satellites, and they were turned to hunting down key groups and organizations. Satellites can do this by thoroughly mapping surface terrain and then by searching for and locating small encampments in remote areas, places where small groups of terrorists gather for training and rehearsing their murderous activities.

It had been known that Osama bin Laden was hiding in mountain areas in Afghanistan, in territory remote and hostile,

A photograph of a suspected Al Qaeda terrorist at a training camp in Afghanistan.

where there are no roads, rivers, or mountain passes. Local tribespeople were used to living and operating in areas where no westerner could travel. There they built hideaways to stack weapons, explosives, and resources capable of supporting small groups of people for several months.

Armed with information about the location of these groups, and with the cooperation of countries working with the United States, the Defense Department conducted a military operation in Afghanistan beginning in late 2001 to seek out and destroy these Al Qaeda bases and to look for Osama bin Laden himself.

The war against terror waged in Afghanistan liberated many of the country's citizens from oppression conducted by the Taliban— a **fanatical** extreme religious body that had taken over control of the country after the Soviet Union withdrew toward the end of the Cold War. Maintaining tight controls over the freedom of individuals in the country, the Taliban had conducted harsh rule and persecuted men, women, and children because of their beliefs.

Many had cooperated with Al Qaeda, and the defeat of terrorism in Afghanistan helped bring about changes in which it would be difficult for terrorism to emerge again. The Defense Department and the U.S. armed forces had conducted a sweep of the country, but many countries around the world were keen to support this action and to do what they could to help give the country a brighter future.

International cooperation was extended with the help of NATO—the North Atlantic Treaty Organization—leading a group of countries forming the International Security Assistance Force (ISAF). ISAF was formed in December 2001 during a conference in Bonn, Germany, which examined the best way to **reconstruct** Afghanistan. NATO took over command of ISAF in August 2003. It was the first mission in NATO's history outside the European and Atlantic area and was a measure of how important the role of the military is in defeating terrorism.

Initially responsible for controlling areas around Kabul, the capital of Afghanistan, by the beginning of 2005 ISAF took over

A soldier from the 29th Infantry Division of the Virginia National Guard stoops to enter and search the home of a suspected Taliban member in Afghanistan on June 4, 2005.

French soldiers of the International Security Assistance Force (ISAF) arrive in Kochi village, near Kabul, Afghanistan, to distribute pens and exercise books to schoolchildren on May 19, 2003.

control of many country areas as well. The role of the military forces is to assist the government in Afghanistan to maintain peace and security so that fair and free elections could be held without threat or violence. By early 2005 about 8,000 troops from 26 NATO countries, ten partners, and one other country (New Zealand) were deployed in the country. Fewer than 150 American troops were in Afghanistan, the rest being provided by NATO and its allies.

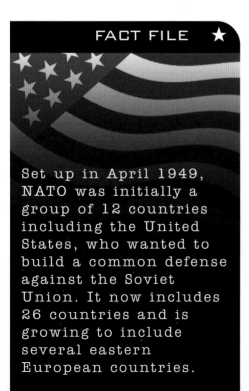

FACT FILE ★

Set up in April 1949, NATO was initially a group of 12 countries including the United States, who wanted to build a common defense against the Soviet Union. It now includes 26 countries and is growing to include several eastern European countries.

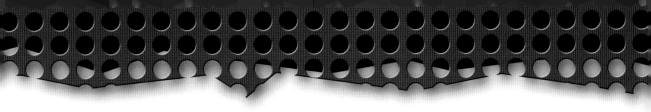

Chapter Ten

The Role of Defense

Operations like those carried out in Afghanistan have changed the way we fight terrorism. In the past, limited actions were carried out by air or naval forces against countries openly boasting their participation in terrible events against ordinary civilians. Before 9/11, it was not possible to invade other countries to attack terrorists without a lot of criticism. Since 9/11 it is no longer possible to stand aside and respect national sovereignty without moving swiftly to put down organizations determined to conduct international murder.

Many people, however, believe that it is dangerous to use military force unless there is no other action that can stop terrorists carrying out their actions. The attack on Iraq in 2003 to topple Saddam Hussein was instigated partly because it was believed the dictator had large stocks of **weapons of mass destruction** (WMD) and partly because he had not complied with United Nations **resolutions**. After extensive searches no WMD were found, but Saddam Hussein was captured, and democratic elections were held in 2005 to select a new leader.

Not all Americans supported the invasion of Iraq. Here, people demonstrate in New York City against President George W. Bush, November 2003.

The use of military force is sometimes unavoidable. It is only because we have a Defense Department that we have the option of using force to oppose the madness of international terrorism. Yet there is a price to pay for that. Some countries believe it is too easy for the United States to use its overwhelming force to achieve by military means what it is unable to negotiate through the State Department.

In reality there is a need for both: a State Department to conduct proper diplomatic negotiations wherever and whenever possible, and a Defense Department capable of securing not only the legitimate freedoms of U.S. citizens but also those of oppressed people who call upon the free world for help. In each case, strength and power bring responsibilities that we use force in a proper manner and only as a last resort. Only in that way can we hope to convince those whose sympathies are with the terrorists that we can allow free speech, respect new ideas, and be a true friend without weakness but tolerance.

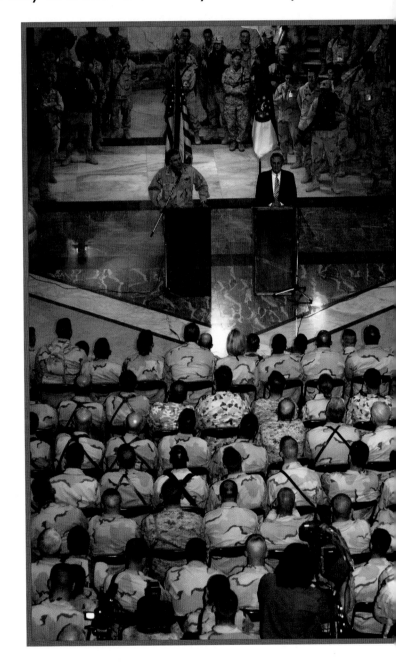

Chairman of the Joint Chiefs of Staff General Richard B. Myers (left) and Secretary of Defense Donald H. Rumsfeld talk to soldiers, Marines, and airmen in the Al Faw Palace at Camp Victory, Iraq, on May 13, 2004.

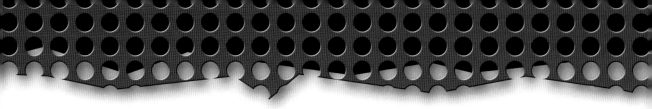

Glossary

administration: a group constituting the political executive in a presidential government

ambassador: a person sent to a foreign country to represent his or her own government

armistice: an agreement made by the opposing sides during a war to stop fighting for a certain amount of time

atrocity: an extremely wicked or cruel act that often involves killing

autocrat: a ruler who has absolute power

bankruptcy: when a person, company, or country is unable to repay its debts

beleaguered: to be harassed or put under pressure from all sides

blitz: a highly destructive or sudden military attack

classified: describes information or documents declared officially secret

colony: a country or region that is occupied by people from a different country and is controlled by that country

commission: a group of people who are instructed to carry out a certain duty

communist: a member of the communist party; someone who believes that the state should control the economy and government of a country

conduit: a means of passage; a channel through which things can pass

custodian: a person or group who looks after or has responsibility for something

dialogue: a conversation between two or more people or governments

dictator: a ruler who has total control over a country and who often gained control by force

diplomat: a person who represents his or her own country's government in a different country

embargo: an official order that forbids something from happening

embassy: the official residence of an ambassador

enclave: a small area enclosed within a larger area or country

environmental pollution: pollution that harms the natural world of plants and animals

ethical: morally right

fanatical: obsessively interested in something

globalization: doing things on a global scale

hijack: to take control of a moving vehicle by force

immigration: the moving into and settling in another country

infiltrate: when people or troops are sent to another country to spy and gain information

liaison: communication between different groups

negotiation: discussion that takes place in order to come to an agreement

oppression: the use of power in a cruel way

radar: equipment that is used to detect things far away and work out their position

reconstruct: to rebuild something that has been destroyed

resolution: an agreement to do something

safe haven: a place of protection or security

stabilize: to make something stable or secure

weapons of mass destruction: weapons capable of causing huge amounts of damage and killing large numbers of people

Further Reading

Binns, Tristan. *The CIA (Government Agencies)*. Sagebrush, 2002

Binns, Tristan. *The FBI (Government Agencies)*. Sagebrush, 2002

Brennan, Kristine. *The Chernobyl Nuclear Disaster (Great Disasters)*. Chelsea House, 2002

Campbell, Geoffrey A. *A Vulnerable America (Lucent Library of Homeland Security)*. Lucent, 2003

Donovan, Sandra. *How Government Works: Protecting America*. Lerner Publishing Group, 2004

Gow, Mary. *Attack on America: The Day the Twin Towers Collapsed (American Disasters)*. Enslow Publishers, 2002

Hasan, Tahara. *Anthrax Attacks Around the World (Terrorist Attacks)*. Rosen Publishing Group, 2003

Katz, Samuel M. *Global Counterstrike: International Counterterrorism (Terrorist Dossiers)*. Lerner Publishing Group, 2004

Katz, Samuel M. *Targeting Terror: Counterterrorist Raids (Terrorist Dossiers)*. Lerner Publishing Group, 2004

Katz, Samuel M. *U.S. Counterstrike: American Counterterrorism (Terrorist Dossiers)*. Lerner Publishing Group, 2004

Margulies, Phillip. *Al-Qaeda: Osama Bin Laden's Army of Terrorists (Inside the World's Most Infamous Terrorist Organizations)*. Rosen Publishing Group, 2003

Marquette, Scott. *America Under Attack (America at War)*. Rourke Publishing LLC, 2003

Morris, Neil. *The Atlas of Islam*. Barron's, 2003

Owen, David. *Hidden Secrets: A Complete History of Espionage and the Technology Used to Support It.* Firefly Books Ltd, 2002

Ritchie, Jason. *Iraq and the Fall of Saddam Hussein.* Oliver Press, 2003

Websites to visit

The Central Intelligence
  Agency:
  www.cia.gov
The Department of Defense:
  www.defenselink.mil
The Department of
  Homeland Security:
  www.dhs.gov
The Federal Bureau of
  Investigation:
  www.fbi.gov
The U.S. Air Force:
  www.af.mil
The U.S. Army
  www.army.mil

The U.S. Coast Guard:
  www.uscg.mil
The U.S. Government
  Official Website:
  www.firstgov.gov
The U.S. Marine Corps:
  www.usmc.mil
The U.S. Navy:
  www.navy.mil
The U.S. Secret Service:
  www.secretservice.gov
The White House:
  www.whitehouse.gov

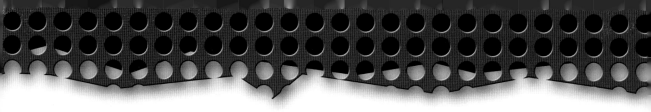

Index